Table of Contents

1 Introduction 1
2 EPC Installer 5
3 Developer Costs 6
4 Transactional Costs 7
5 Total System Price 8
6 Margin versus Overhead 10
7 Summary 12
8 References 15
Appendix A. EPC Installer Direct and Indirect Corporate Costs 16
Appendix B. Developer Direct and Indirect Corporate Costs 18
Appendix C. Breakdown of Direct Costs and Margins 20

List of Figures

Figure 1. Organization chart of benchmarked business model..3
Figure 2. Third-party residential system direct cost breakdown in 2012................................8
Figure 3. Third-party commercial system direct cost breakdown in 2012...............................9
Figure 4. Segmented residential PV system costs ("other soft costs" broken out).................12
Figure 5. Segmented commercial PV system costs ("other soft costs" broken out)................12
Figure 6. Percentage of residential PV capacity installed as third-party systems in select states . 13

List of Tables

Table 1. Pro-Forma Model Assumptions 10
Table 2. Summary of Pro-Forma Cash Flows to Tax-Equity Investor and System Developer..........11
Table A-1. Residential EPC Installer Direct and Indirect Corporate Costs in 2012.............16
Table A-2. Commercial EPC Installer Direct and Indirect Corporate Costs in 2012.............17
Table B-1. Developer Direct and Indirect Corporate Costs in 2012 18
Table C-1. Breakdown of Direct Costs and Margins in 2012 20

1 Introduction

The median price of residential and commercial photovoltaic (PV) systems fell in 2012 and has fallen 8 of the last 10 years, according to research from the Lawrence Berkeley National Laboratory (Barbose et al. 2013). Much of this price reduction has been attributed to reductions in hardware costs, such as module price, which has fallen by 78% in the past 10 years (Barbose et al. 2013). Non-hardware costs (or "soft costs") have thus become a larger percentage of total system costs, and more efforts have been made to understand and reduce them. In the National Renewable Energy Laboratory (NREL) soft cost benchmarking report (Ardani et al. 2012), 55%-88% of benchmarked 2010 soft costs were categorized in the unsegmented category of "other soft costs," leaving a significant portion not well defined or understood. This report attempts to better quantify the "other soft costs" by focusing on financing, overhead, and profit for residential and commercial PV installations. The results are incorporated in the second edition of the soft cost benchmarking report (Friedman et al. 2013).[1]

Financing, overhead, and profit can become particularly complicated when systems are financed through a third party, such as through solar leases and power purchase agreements (PPAs), in which there are more parties involved in the transaction than are involved in a direct sale. Because third-party financing has become the dominant business model in much of the United States [responsible for approximately 68% of all U.S. residential systems installed during 2012 (Kann 2013)], it is even more important to understand the costs associated with this business model.

Before quantifying these costs we will define some financial terms in relation to the cost of a PV system; these terms are typically used in financial statements to provide information on the financial position of a company.[2] PV system costs include costs directly associated with building the system and the long-term, total cost that a business incurs related to the system (i.e., all indirect costs). The direct costs of a project can be best compared to the "cost of goods sold" (COGS) line item in a company's income statement, or the direct costs attributable to the production of goods sold. In the case of a PV system, these costs include the hardware (e.g., modules, inverters, and racking) and all labor and other costs associated with building the specific project (e.g., installation labor, system design, and permitting). The COGS plus a gross margin equals the price of a project, or the revenue a company receives. For example, if the COGS of a PV system is $4/W and the gross margin is 25%, the gross profit would be $1/W and the system price would be $5/W (or $5/W in total revenue to the company).

The indirect "operating" fixed costs to a business can be best compared to selling, general, and administrative expenses (SG&A).[3] SG&A can be defined as the costs of operating a business not

---

[1] Some of the assumptions in this report differ from the assumptions in Friedman et al. (2013), thus the results between the two reports are not directly comparable. See Friedman et al. (2013) for an explanation of how the numbers in this report were translated into the other report.

[2] Many of these terms are defined in the general accepted accounting principles (GAAP), which are a common set of accounting principles, standards, and procedures used for U.S. companies in their financial statements. They may have slightly different definitions from those above; however, they are generally consistent in spirit.

[3] SG&A, overhead, and non-direct costs are all terms used loosely to describe similar costs on an income statement. Generally, although not always, they refer to the ongoing costs of operating a business.

related to the production of a good. Examples of this would include an installer's office space, sales staff, and its human resources (HR) department. In an efficient, long-term business model, the margin over COGS should equal SG&A plus a sustainable operating profit.[4] Operating profit allows a company to return money back to investors or make strategic investments. For example, if the gross profit of a PV system is $1/W and a company's SG&A spread over all its sold systems is $0.5/W, then the company would have an operating profit of $0.5/W.

In growing, hypercompetitive businesses or over short time horizons, a company might not be able to fund SG&A through revenue fully; however, if SG&A is not fully funded in the long term, such a company would likely go out of business.

The benchmarking analysis in Friedman et al. (2013) generally includes SG&A and COGS.[5] For example, an engineer's time associated with design of a particular system is classified as COGS, but not the engineer's time associated with designing systems that do not move forward. Gross profit, or—in the case of a growing or unhealthy company—existing corporate cash, must cover SG&A. Therefore, SG&A must be discussed in parallel with gross profit.

To gain a better understanding of all the costs associated with building a PV system, we modeled a prevalent business arrangement that captures the direct and indirect costs of a company operating a business that installs residential and commercial PV systems. To build the model, we conducted in-depth interviews with members of financing departments at large PV installation companies on the subjects of third-party financing and overhead costs, and we collected data from industry participants' corporate public filings. There are many different business models in the PV marketplace,[6] but we chose the business structure in Figure 1 for three primary reasons: to show the additional cost categories of third-party installations, to better represent the specific costs of each activity by avoiding a vertically integrated structure, and to demonstrate a business model that is currently common in the marketplace.

---

[4] There are other, non-operating costs to a company that concern the financing and investment of a company. We focus only on operating costs.

[5] SG&A expenses are ineligible inclusions in the cost basis reported to the Treasury Department or the Internal Revenue Service for purposes of the 1603 cash grant or investment tax credit. However, some COGS costs are ineligible, such as permanent loan fees, syndication costs, and roof repair. It should be noted that the cost plus margin approach detailed in this report is not the only way in which the basis of a project is reported to the Treasury Department (e.g., 1603) or the Internal Revenue Service (e.g., ITC), particularly in cases involving related parties. As summarized in "Evaluating Cost Basis for Solar Photovoltaic Properties (Treasury 2011)," the Treasury Department accepts three different ways of calculating the "fair market value": the cost approach, "based on the actual cost to build the property"; the market approach, "based on sales of comparable properties"; and the income approach, "based on the discounted value of future cash flows generated by and appropriately allocable to the eligible property." In the latter two approaches, cash flow is more relevant than cost.

[6] For example, SolarCity acts as the lead generator/sales staff, the EPC installer, and the developer, while Clean Power Finance works with partners to perform sales and installation, such as Real Goods Solar. There are also several different financing models other than the sale leaseback approach, such as the partnership-flip structure and the inverted lease structure.

Organization Chart of Benchmarked Business Model

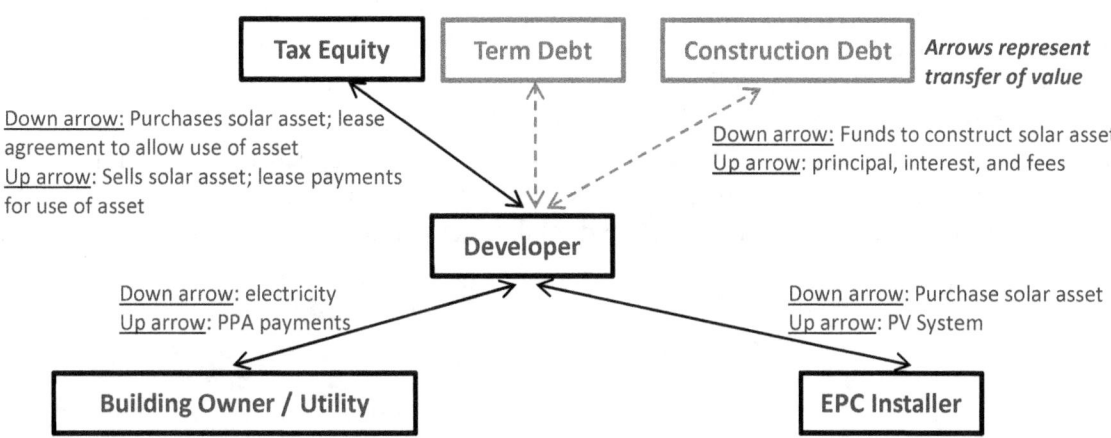

Figure 1. Organization chart of benchmarked business model7

In this business structure, the developer signs a PPA with a building owner, contracts the construction of the system with a separate engineering, procurement, and construction (EPC) installer, and finances a portfolio of systems (we assume 10 MW of residential or commercial systems) through a sale-leaseback arrangement with a tax-equity investor. For larger, non-residential projects, a separate financier may be brought on to fund construction of these assets before they are sold to the tax-equity investor at the projects' placed-in-service dates. Further, non-recourse term debt may be raised to fund part of the portfolio, depending largely on the tax equity investor's minimum investment size threshold; in other words, the debt must not exceed an amount that would reduce the tax equity portion to a level below that threshold.[8]

Because some companies currently in the marketplace are vertically integrated, many of these functions can be performed by the same participant or handled at different points of the value chain. For example, developers may perform lead generation and sales, or the EPC installers may accomplish this task. This benchmark attempts to characterize one of many possible business models—one in which the market participants are *not* vertically integrated but are separate entities.[9] Inputs to and design of this model are based on discussions from multiple industry participants involved in third-party PV financing as well as data from corporate public filings and vetting and review by external stakeholders.

The previously discussed portfolio of assets includes *direct costs* in three categories: (1) direct project costs, such as PV hardware costs, installation labor, and permitting fees; (2) transactional costs, which include fees by parties other than the EPC installer or system developer to arrange financing; and (3) EPC installer and system developer corporate costs, defined as staff time

---

[7] The labels "up" and "down" represent the direction in which the benefits flow between the relevant two parties.
[8] Tax equity investors typically require a higher rate of return when subordinating themselves to debt and making a smaller investment. The unlevered (i.e., no debt) rate of return for tax equity is estimated to be between 8% and 10%, versus a levered financial arrangement in which tax equity requires 10% to 12%.
[9] While there is potential for cost reductions through vertical integration of the EPC installer and integrator, each has a separate value proposition. Therefore, if the companies operate efficiently, they should have the same cost structure before and after consolidation.

associated with specific projects. Appendix C summarizes these direct costs (plus margin), and Appendix A and Appendix B detail the direct corporate costs of the EPC installer and system developer, respectively. In addition to direct costs, the EPC installer and system developer have indirect costs associated with the previously discussed portfolio of assets. Appendix A and Appendix B also summarize these indirect corporate costs (in red), including business expenses, such as rent and office supplies and staff time not directly associated with projects. The results should be treated as representative of general trends in 2012 and not specific to any company. The following sections detail the costs listed in the tables through the following categories: EPC installer, developer costs, transactional costs, and total system price.

2 EPC Installer

The EPC installer in the model is assumed to build 12 MW of residential or commercial PV systems per year (in contrast to the 10 MW[10] of systems in the sold portfolio and the 70 MW of systems developed by the developer).[11] Office rent, equipment and supplies, insurance, taxes, vehicles, dues, and memberships, as well as corporate professional services such as accountants and lawyers, are estimated as non-staff corporate overhead, a subset of SG&A. In addition, estimates are made of staff expenses, such as corporate positions (CEO, HR, legal), sales and marketing, design and engineering, and project managers; percentages are also determined to proportionally allocate costs between those that are directly and indirectly related to projects. Finally, a 35% increase is added to base salaries to account for benefits, FICA,[12] and salary bonuses. These costs for residential systems total $3.2 million, or $0.27/W, of indirect costs (i.e., SG&A, overhead) and $2.2 million, or $0.19/W, of direct costs (Appendix A, Table A-1). These costs for commercial systems total $2.2 million, or $0.18/W, of indirect costs (i.e., SG&A, overhead) and $1.8 million, or $0.15/W, of direct costs (Appendix A, Table A-2).

---

[10] The 2 MW difference between the EPC installer volume of 12 MW and the portfolio size of 10 MW includes separate transactions, such as host-owned systems.

[11] The sales volume (MW) by EPC installer and integrator, and the size of portfolio, are indicative of companies and projects in the underlying data used to generate report.

[12] FICA is the Federal Insurance Contributions Act payroll tax that funds Social Security and Medicare.

3 Developer Costs

The developer is assumed to install 70 MW of residential or commercial PV systems per year. Like the EPC installer, office rent, equipment and supplies, insurance, taxes, vehicles, dues, and memberships, as well as corporate professional service such as accountants and lawyers, are estimated as corporate overhead. However, it is also assumed that consultants, recruiters, and lobbyists are necessary, as well as the cost of purchasing a billing system, which is prorated over a 5-year period.

There are also significantly more operational requirements at the corporate level for a developer than an EPC installer. In addition to a larger corporate staff of executives and HR, as well as a legal team, there is also a finance team, which handles corporate treasury duties, project finance arrangements, compliance, and accounting. There are also sales, marketing, and EPC sales management teams that develop PPA customer portfolios. A design and engineering department, supply chain management team, rebate interconnection team, and project management team shepherd the PV projects from design, procurement of equipment, and construction of project to system interconnection to the grid. Finally, once the PV projects are in operation, the software/IT department (which also handles general corporate needs and customer acquisition) and the customer service department monitor, bill, and interact with customers. Percentages were determined to proportionally allocate costs directly and indirectly related to projects. A 35% increase is again added to salaries to account for benefits, FICA, and salary bonuses. These costs total $53.2 million, or $0.76/W, of indirect costs (i.e., SG&A, overhead) and $16.5 million, or $0.24/W, of direct costs, for both commercial and residential systems (Appendix B).

4 Transactional Costs

Structuring financing for a PV asset involves arranging, negotiating, and contracting agreements between two or more parties. These transactions are designed to allocate the benefits of a PV system to entities that can use them, at the lowest cost possible. The tax-equity investor is brought into the deal to utilize the investment tax credit and depreciation benefits; debt is raised to fund a portion of the project at a lower cost than the rate of return required for equity; and, in the case of large commercial systems with long construction timelines, construction debt is raised to minimize risk to the tax-equity investor during construction. All of these companies serve a purpose, but they come at a cost.

Before an arrangement can be put in place, the purchasers of the assets (tax-equity) must validate what they are buying from the developer.[13] It was assumed that an auditor is hired to assess the residential portfolio; in a portfolio of commercial systems, use of independent engineers is assumed. Lawyers on both sides of the transaction (tax-equity and developer) are needed to negotiate the necessary contracts, although the developer typically pays both fees. Accountants are also often necessary to validate the financial records of a project and/or developer. Our modeled results for professional service costs, summarized in Appendix C, yielded $0.05/W for residential and $0.06/W for commercial.

Banks that offer term debt typically charge a fee to set up the transaction. In addition, in the case of construction debt for commercial projects, an arranging fee is charged as well as interest on the loan during construction (which can be added to the cost basis of a project for tax purposes). Our modeled results for debt fees (and interest), summarized in Appendix C, yielded $0.04/W for residential and $0.08/W for commercial.

There are also provisions that developers must make to minimize the risk to investors and PPA customers in the transaction. The value of extended inverter warranties that last the life of the contract, and system production guarantees made to the end-user, which are all often necessary for third-party ownership, come at a cost.[14] In addition, debt providers often require that money is set aside to cover payments (debt service reserve) in case of revenue variability, and tax-equity investors often require that developers set aside money to cover Operations and Maintenance (O&M) costs (O&M reserve). These reserves are not eligible for inclusion in a project's cost basis, but funds are still necessary. Our modeled results for the additional costs (without reserves), summarized in Appendix C, yielded $0.12/W for residential and $0.10/W commercial. Our modeled results for the capital reserves yielded $0.05/W for both residential and commercial systems.

In total, the transaction costs to set up and construct a 10-MW residential portfolio and a 10-MW commercial portfolio, summarized in Appendix C, were modeled to be $0.21/W and $0.24/W, respectively (excluding capital reserves).

---

[13] This model assumes that the integrator, after purchasing the system from the EPC installer, immediately sells the system to the tax-equity provider.

[14] Some of these costs are also borne when the system is sold directly to the end user.

5 Total System Price

Project costs such as hardware, construction labor,[15] and permitting are based on NREL's bottom-up reported benchmarks, as detailed in Feldman et al. (2013). When added to liability insurance during construction and the direct EPC installer staff costs summarized above and in Appendix A, they total $2.92/W for residential PV systems and $2.50/W for commercial systems (Appendix C). A margin of 20% is charged for residential systems and 10% for commercial systems, making the system price to the developer $3.50/W for residential ($0.58/W margin) and $2.76/W for commercial ($0.25/W margin). The margin on a commercial system is typically less than that of a residential system as overhead is cheaper on a per watt basis and there is more competition, driving prices lower.

The developer also has staff costs directly related to the project, such as design and engineering, project management, and sales. Once they have structured the financial transaction, the developer sells the system to the tax-equity provider, with a 15% margin on all their direct costs associated with the project (including items purchased from the EPC installer).[16] For this given corporate structure, adding all costs and margins together, a residential PV system would have a total system price of $4.52/W, and a commercial system would have a system price of $3.66/W. Adding cash reserves of $0.05/W (residential) and $0.05/W (commercial), the amount increases to $4.58/W (residential) and $3.71/W (commercial) (Figure 2 and Figure 3).

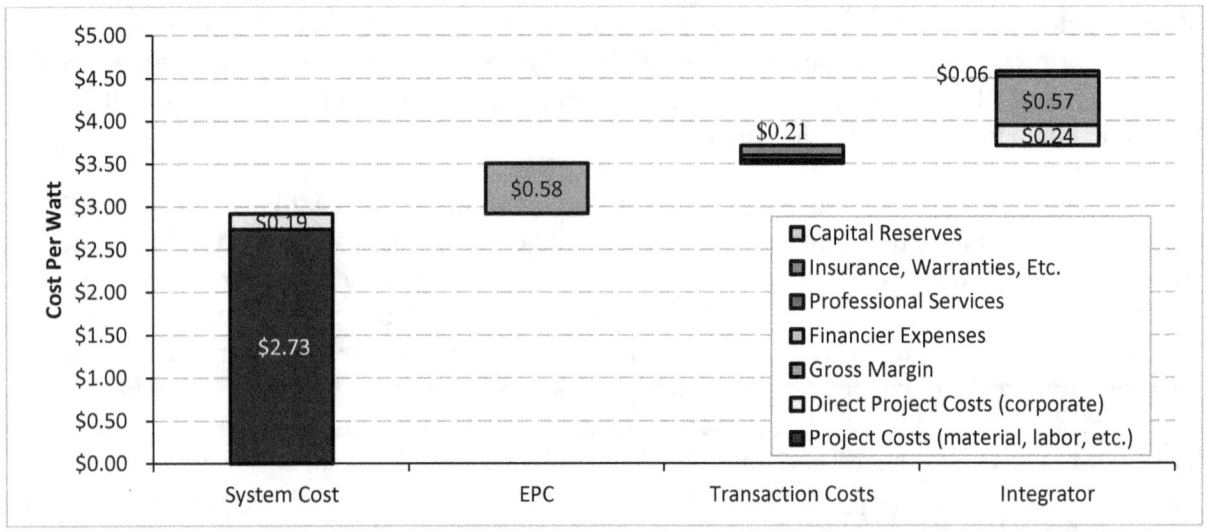

Figure 2. Third-party residential system direct cost breakdown in 2012

---

[15] In Feldman et al. (2013), construction labor's marked-up costs (to account for FICA, etc.) are included in its overhead costs, which are calculated differently in this report. Therefore, this report added an additional 35% line-item cost to account for this discrepancy.

[16] This also may be labeled a "development fee." The Internal Revenue Service usually allows a development fee at a maximum of 15% of the cost of the project to the integrator.

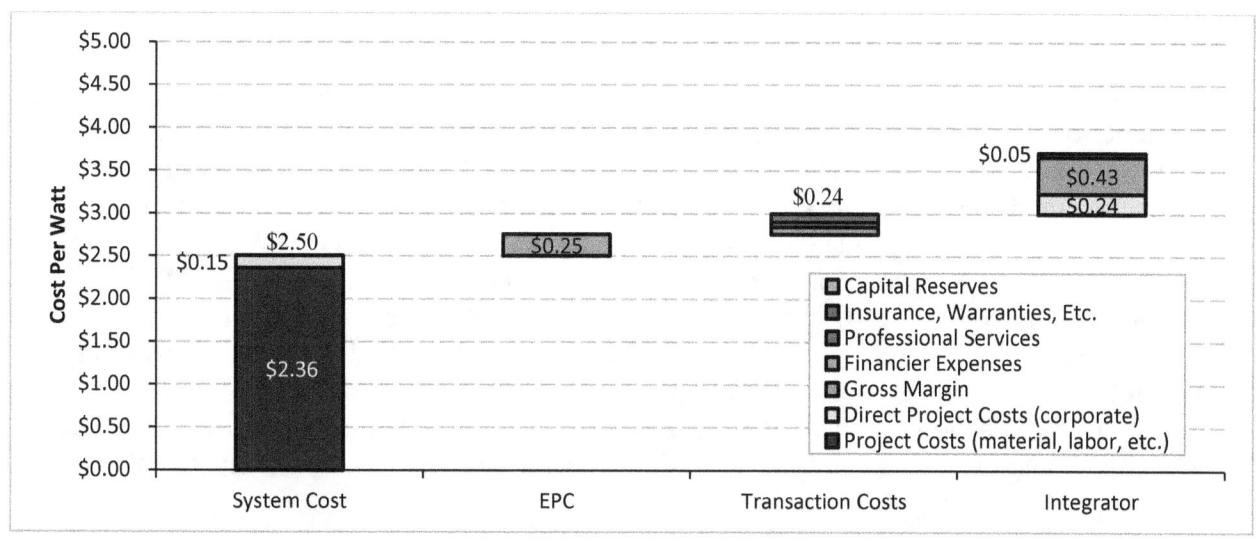

Figure 3. Third-party commercial system direct cost breakdown in 2012

6 Margin Versus Overhead

As mentioned previously, overhead costs are typically funded in a company through the margin it charges on the cost of its product. In the case of the EPC installer, the profit margins charged for residential and commercial systems were $0.58/W and $0.25/W, respectively, for the transaction modeled (Appendix C). EPC installer indirect corporate costs (i.e., SG&A) for a residential system were calculated in Appendix A to be $0.27/W (the $0.19/W direct costs are paid from the sale of the assets), which would provide a positive operating profit of $0.32/W (an operating margin of 9%). EPC installer indirect corporate costs (i.e., SG&A) for a commercial system were calculated in Appendix A to be $0.18/W (the $0.15/W direct costs are paid from the sale of the assets), which would provide a positive operating profit of $0.06/W (an operating margin of 2%). The lower operating margin for a commercial system can be attributed to the necessity of charging a lower system price due to such factors as increased competition and lower electricity pricing (compared to the residential market).

The developer also charges a mark-up in its sale of the asset to the tax-equity investor in a sale-leaseback transaction, which was calculated in Appendix C to be $0.57/W for a residential system and $0.43/W for a commercial system. These fees are $0.19/W and $0.33/W less than the $0.76/W of indirect corporate costs by the developer for residential and commercial systems, respectively ($0.24/W of direct costs are paid from the sale of the assets) (Appendix B). However, developers typically also receive money after a system is placed in service through partial ownership or leasing of the equipment. Therefore, they are more concerned with a PV project pro-forma satisfying its requirements to stakeholders than the cost of a project. In other words, a developer's priority is for the PPA revenues and tax benefits (and any other benefits) to provide the tax-equity investor, debt holder, and other equity holders with their required returns.

In order to validate the cost model benchmarks in Appendix C, a pro-forma was created for a residential system, with consistent assumptions summarized in Table 1.

Table 1. Pro-Forma Model Assumptions

System size	5.1 kW$_{DC}$	
Total system price	$4.52/W$_{DC}$	
	Term	Tax-equity
Capital structure (%)	40%	60%
Capital structure ($/W)	$1.81	$2.71
Term debt interest rate	7.0%	
Term of loan	12 years	
Tax-equity investor required	12.0%	
Production factor	1,750 kWh/kW	
Annual degradation factor	0.5%	
PPA price	$0.21/kWh	
PPA term	20 years	
O&M Costs	$23.50/kW per year	
PPA and O&M cost escalator	3.5% per annum	
ITC Rate	30%	
Federal & state depreciation	5 year MACRS	
State tax rate	8%	

Federal tax rate	35%
Model assumes developer purchases project from tax-equity investor in year 6 for 20% of the original system price. No assumed state incentives.	

The pro-forma modeled cash flows, over the 20-year life of the PPA, to the tax-equity investor and the developer are summarized in Table 2.

Table 2. Summary of Pro-Forma Cash Flows to Tax-Equity Investor and System Developer

	Net present value [17] ($/W)
Tax-equity investor (lessor)	
Initial investment (Year 0)	-$2.71
Lease payments (Y1-Y6)	$1.41
Buyout (Y6)	$0.46
Total revenue	$1.87
Interest (Y1-Y6)	-$0.22
State taxes (Y1-Y6)	$0.17[18]
Federal taxes (Y1-Y6)	$0.70
Debt principle (Y1-Y6)	-$1.18
Total expenses	-$0.51
ITC (Y0)	$1.36
NPV of after tax cash flow	$0.00
After tax IRR	*12.0%*
Developer (lessee)	
Electricity revenue (Y1-Y20)	$2.72
Total revenue	**$2.72**
Buyout (Y6)	-$0.39
Operating expenses (O&M, insurance, management) (Y1-Y20)	-$0.18
Lease payments to tax-equity (Y1-Y6)	-$1.30
Total expenses	**-$1.87**
Operating profit (revenue – expense)	**$0.85**
Margin from sale to tax-equity investor (Y0), from Appendix	**$0.57**
Project cash flow (operating profit + margin from sale)	**$1.43**
Developer indirect costs, from Appendix B	**-$0.76**
Total developer cash flow (project cash flow – indirect	**$0.67**

As presented in Table 2, the project modeled in the pro-forma was able to satisfy all debt and equity stakeholders and provide the developer with a net present value of $0.85 /W over a 20-year PPA life (assuming a 15% discount rate). When accounting for both the margin on the sale of the asset and the profit from operations, the developer achieves $1.43/W in value, or $0.67/W more than all indirect corporate costs.

---

[17] The tax-equity investor's cash flows are discounted to present value at a rate of 12%; the integrator's cash flows are discounted to present value at a rate of 15%. These discount rates are based on the required rate of return necessary, as indicated by current market conditions

[18] Federal and state tax expenses are positive due to the PV asset's depreciation schedule and interest expense.

7 Summary

In this business model, residential systems' "other soft costs" contribute $1.79/W out of a total $4.52/W (40%), which is further segmented in Figure 4. Commercial systems' "other soft costs" contribute $1.14/W out of a total $3.66/W (36%), which is further segmented in Figure 5.

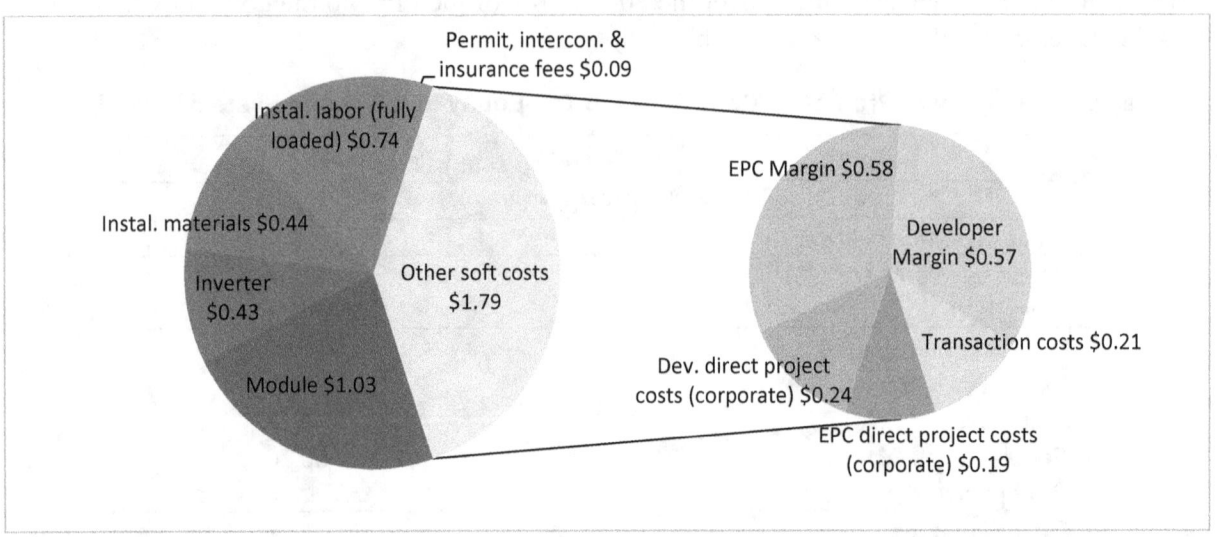

Figure 4. Segmented residential PV system costs ("other soft costs" broken out)

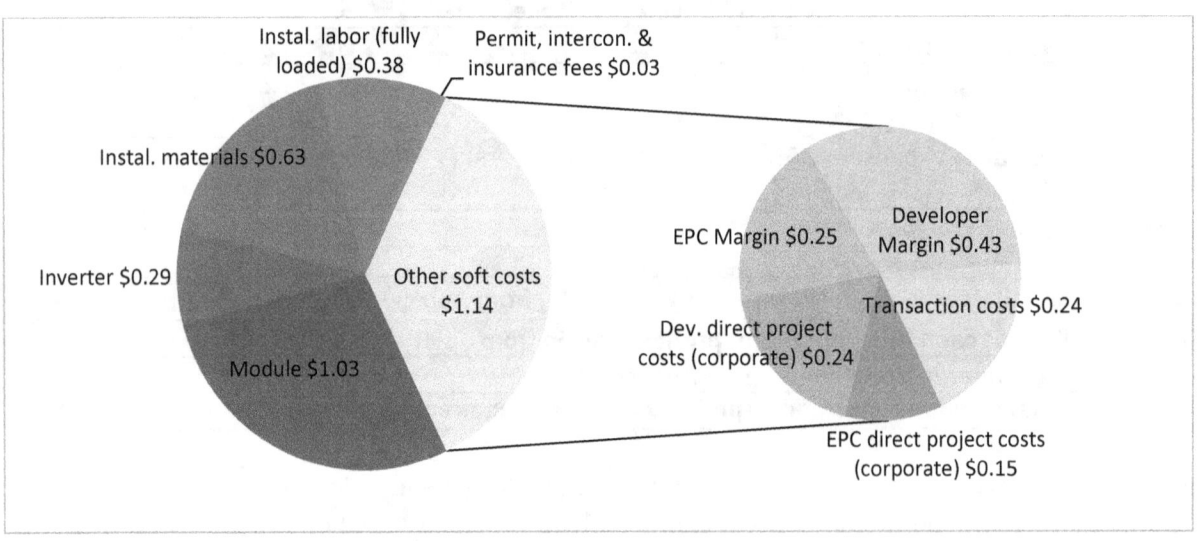

Figure 5. Segmented commercial PV system costs ("other soft costs" broken out)

Of the "other soft costs," third-party-ownership-related costs—namely the addition of the developer's margin (which partially covers its indirect costs) and transaction costs—add $0.78/W to a residential portfolio ($0.57/W developer margin and $0.21/W transactions costs, see Appendix A) and $0.67/W to a commercial portfolio ($0.43/W developer margin and

$0.24/W transactions costs, see Appendix A).[19] However, this ignores three of the main benefits of third-party financing arrangements. First, third-party financiers offer additional services not provided by direct ownership. A customer does not have to dedicate the resources to purchasing a system, worry about its O&M, or apply for and receive any incentives (ITC, state/regional rebates, RECs, etc.). Second, while there are transactional costs associated with multiple parties financing projects, this is done to (1) properly allocate the benefits (e.g., a tax-equity provider can utilize the tax credits and depreciation deductions) and (2) lower the capital cost (e.g., term debt has a lower required rate of return than an equity provider); these effectively lower the cost of electricity, which has more economic impact to a consumer than the upfront cost. Third, third-party businesses have gained significant market share in the United States, driving a considerable amount of PV demand. Figure 6 shows the percentage of PV capacity installed as third-party systems in four select states.

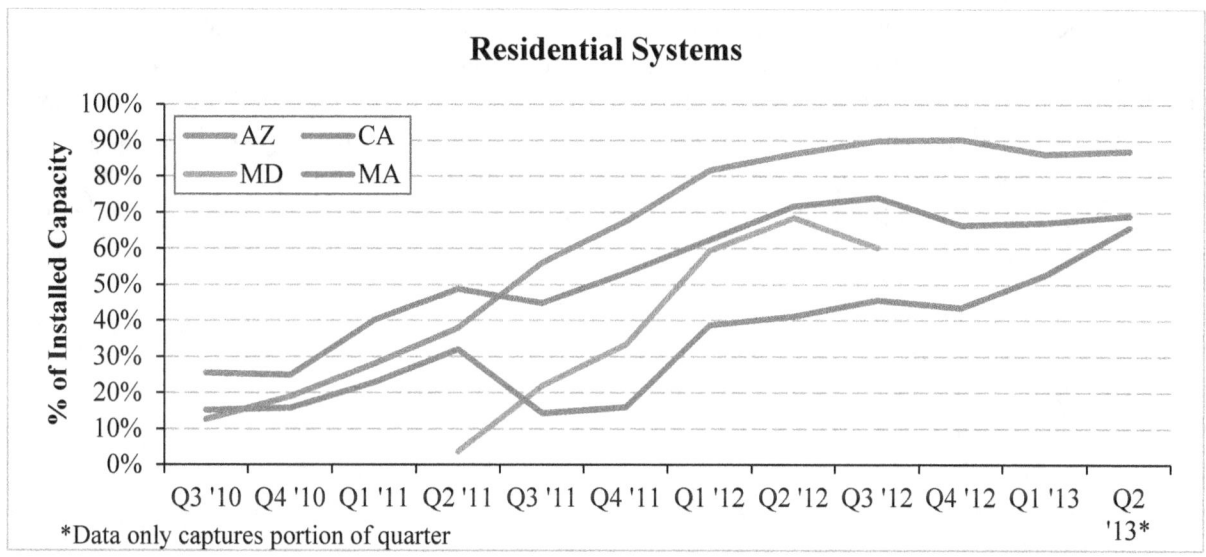

Figure 6. Percentage of residential PV capacity installed as third-party systems in select states

Without this volume of third-party customers, EPC installers are significantly less likely to operate efficiently, which will cause overhead costs to increase. For example, in Arizona, approximately 90% of the systems installed during 2012 and through the first half of 2013 were third-party owned. Without the third-party option, it is likely that fewer customers would be willing to purchase PV systems (e.g., due to first cost barriers), and the market would shrink considerably, possibly driving up overhead costs to EPC installers on a per-watt basis. The model calculates that the indirect overhead for an EPC installer who builds 12 MW of residential

---

[19] The direct costs incurred by the integrator are not included in this calculation because they would also be required for a direct sale. In that situation, those activities would most likely be handled by an EPC installer instead. Also, while there is potential for cost reductions through vertical integration of the EPC installer and integrator, each has a separate value proposition. Therefore, if the companies operate efficiently, they will have the same cost structure before and after consolidation.

systems a year is $3.2 million, or $0.27/W. If the EPC installer's sales volume decreased, overhead costs could increase dramatically.[20]

As discussed, differences in companies' sales volume can have a large impact on indirect costs.[21] This may partially explain the differences in measurements of system pricing. For example, the above model estimates that, in 2012, the installed price of a residential system was $4.52/W, compared to the median reported price of $5.22/W calculated by *Tracking the Sun VI* (Barbose et al. 2013) based on installer-reported system prices. If the EPC installer and system developers who contributed information to *Tracking the Sun VI* have median sale volumes that are lower than those in the model, but have the same costs, they would have higher costs per watt. Due to these higher costs, EPC installers and system developers may need to charge higher gross margins, thus raising the system price. In addition, gross margins may be higher than those modeled in areas of the United States because of market factors, such as high local electricity prices or lack of competition, translating into higher profits to the EPC installer and system developers.[22] As the industry matures and the U.S. PV market grows (as it is projected to do in the next few years), and as companies with uncompetitive business models exit the marketplace, overhead costs and margins will come down on their own. However, because of third-party ownership's value propositions, as outlined above, developers may still be a necessary part of a transaction, regardless of price.

---

[20] Practically speaking, an EPC installer would cut its overhead with a decrease in sales; however, because there are large economies of scale in overhead, their costs would most likely still be higher, on a per-watt basis.

[21] Sales volume can also impact direct costs through stronger purchasing power.

[22] Developers may also be able to charge higher margins based on their method of reporting "fair market value" to the IRS or Treasury. In instances in which fair market value is based on the future cash flows of a project, instead of the cost, margin is not reported. However, the ability of a developer to charge high margins is still dependent on lack of competition, high electricity prices, and related party transactions.

8 References

Ardani, K.; Barbose, G.; Margolis, R.; Wiser, R.; Feldman, D.; Ong, S. (2012). *Benchmarking Non-Hardware Balance of System (Soft) Costs for U.S. Photovoltaic Systems Using a Data-Driven Analysis from PV Installer Survey Results.* NREL/TP-7A20-56806. Golden, CO: National Renewable Energy Laboratory.

Barbose, G.; Darghouth, N.; Wiser, R. (2013). *Tracking the Sun VI: An Historical Summary of the Installed Cost of Photovoltaics in the United States from 1998 to 2012.* Berkeley, CA: Lawrence Berkeley National Laboratory.

Feldman D.; Barbose, G.; Margolis, R.; Darghouth, N.; James, T.; Weaver, S.; Goodrich, A.; Wiser. R. (2013). *Photovoltaic System Pricing Trends: Historical, Recent, and Near-Term Projections. 2013 Edition.* NREL/PR-6A20-60207. Golden, CO: National Renewable Energy Laboratory.

Friedman, B.; Ardani, K.; Feldman, D.; Margolis, R.; Citron, R.; Zuboy, J. (2013). *Benchmarking Non-Hardware Balance-of-System (Soft) Costs for U.S. Photovoltaic Systems, Using a Bottom-Up Approach and Installer Survey – Second Edition.* NREL/TP-6A20-60412. Golden, CO: National Renewable Energy Laboratory.

Kann, S. (2013). *U.S. Residential Solar PV Financing: The Vendor, Installer and Financier Landscape, 2013–2016.* Boston: GTM Research.

Treasury Department. (June 2011). "Evaluating Cost Basis for Solar Photovoltaic Properties." Accessed August 27, 2013:

Appendix A. EPC Installer Direct and Indirect Corporate Costs

Table A-1. Residential EPC Installer Direct and Indirect Corporate Costs in 2012

Indirect Corporate Overhead						
Business Expenses					$/year	$/W
Rent (98 sq ft/person)	$13.75/sq ft				$60,420	$0.01
Office expenses (equipment, supplies, maintenance, phones)	$5,000/person				$225,000	$0.02
Corp. professional service (accountants, lawyers)					$258,120	$0.02
Insurance					$30,000	$0.00
Other (business taxes, bank fees)					$20,000	$0.00
Vehicle fees (lease, gas, insurance)					$20,000	$0.00
Dues and memberships					$20,000	$0.00
Staff Expenses						
	Base Salary (unburdened) / person	# of employees	Employee per MW installed	Time **not** assoc. w/direct proj. cost	(Base Salary + Benefits) × % of time	
Corporate (senior)	$200,000	2	0.17	100%	$540,000	$0.05
Corporate (junior)	$55,000	3	0.25	80%	$178,200	$0.01
Design and engineering	$65,000	12	1.00	50%	$526,500	$0.04
Sales and marketing	$80,000	24	2.00	50%	$1,296,000	$0.11
Project managers	$75,000	4	0.33	10%	$40,500	$0.00
Total employees		**45**	**3.75**		**$2,581,200**	**$0.22**
Benefits, FICA, bonus (added to base salary)	35%					
Total indirect corporate costs (staff + business expenses)					**$3,214,740**	**$0.27**
Direct Corporate Overhead						
Staff Expenses						
	Base Salary (unburdened) / person	# of employees	Employee per MW installed	Time assoc. w/direct proj. cost	(Base Salary + Benefits) × % of time	
Corporate (junior)	$55,000	3		20%	$44,550	$0.00
Design and engineering	$65,000	12		50%	$526,500	$0.04
Sales and marketing	$80,000	24		50%	$1,296,000	$0.11
Project managers	$75,000	4		90%	$364,500	$0.03
Total direct corporate staff costs					**$2,231,550**	**$0.19**
MW installed by EPC installer per year					12	

Table A-2. Commercial EPC Installer Direct and Indirect Corporate Costs in 2012

Indirect Corporate Overhead						
Business Expenses					**$/year**	**$/W**
Rent (98 sq ft/person)	$13.75/sq ft				$41,586	$0.00
Office expenses (equipment, supplies, maintenance, phones)	$5,000/person				$154,865	$0.01
Corp. professional service (accountants, lawyers)					$175,760	$0.01
Insurance					$30,000	$0.00
Other (business taxes, bank fees)					$20,000	$0.00
Vehicle fees (lease, gas, insurance)					$20,000	$0.00
Dues and memberships					$20,000	$0.00
Staff Expenses						
	Base Salary (unburdened) / person	# of employees	Employee per MW installed	Time _not_ assoc. w/direct proj. cost	(Base Salary + Benefits) × % of time	
Corporate (senior)	$200,000	3	0.23	100%	$760,247	$0.06
Corporate (junior)	$55,000	2	0.18	80%	$125,441	$0.01
Design and engineering	$65,000	7	0.59	50%	$308,851	$0.03
Sales and marketing	$80,000	8	0.70	50%	$456,148	$0.04
Project managers	$75,000	11	0.88	10%	$106,910	$0.01
Total employees		**31**	**2.58**		**$1,757,597**	**$0.15**
Benefits, FICA, bonus (added to base salary)	35%					
Total indirect corporate costs (staff + business expenses)					**$2,219,808**	**$0.18**
Direct Corporate Overhead						
Staff Expenses						
	Base Salary (unburdened) / person	# of employees	Employee per MW installed	Time assoc. w/direct proj. cost	(Base Salary + Benefits) × % of time	
Corporate (junior)	$55,000	2		20%	$31,360	$0.00
Design and engineering	$65,000	7		50%	$308,851	$0.03
Sales and marketing	$80,000	8		50%	$456,148	$0.04
Project managers	$75,000	11		90%	$962,188	$0.08
Total direct corporate staff costs					**$1,758,547**	**$0.15**
MW installed by EPC installer per year					12	

Appendix B. Developer Direct and Indirect Corporate Costs

Table B-1. Developer Direct and Indirect Corporate Costs in 2012

Indirect Corporate Overhead						
Business Expenses					**$/year**	**$/W**
Rent (98 sq ft/person)	$28.92/sq ft				$1,519,262	$0.02
Office expenses (equipment, supplies, maintenance, phones)	$5,000/person				$2,689,928	$0.04
Corp. professional service (accountants, lawyers, consultants, recruiting, lobbying)					$4,353,589	$0.06
Insurance					$30,000	$0.00
Other (business taxes, bank fees)					$20,000	$0.00
Vehicle fees (lease, gas, insurance)					$913,172	$0.01
Dues and memberships					$20,000	$0.00
Billing system (prorated over 5 years)					$100,000	$0.00
Staff Expenses						
	Base Salary (unburdened) / person	# of employees	Employees per MW installed	Time _not_ assoc. w/direct proj. cost	(Base Salary + Benefits) × % of time	
Corporate - senior (c-level, HR & legal)	$185,000	22.5	0.32	100%	$5,611,798	$0.08
Corporate - junior (c-level, HR & legal)	$75,000	13.8	0.20	100%	$1,400,033	$0.02
Finance - senior (treasury, project finance, accounting, compliance)	$185,000	10.4	0.15	100%	$2,590,061	$0.04
Finance - junior (treasury, project finance, accounting, compliance)	$75,000	34.6	0.49	100%	$3,500,082	$0.05
Design and engineering	$75,000	66.4	0.95	50%	$3,359,415	$0.05
Supply chain	$75,000	6.9	0.10	100%	$700,016	$0.01
Software/IT	$85,000	49.3	0.70	100%	$5,656,103	$0.08
Rebate/interconnection	$75,000	20.4	0.29	100%	$2,065,109	$0.03
Project management	$75,000	42.5	0.61	10%	$430,231	$0.01
Customer service	$75,000	17.0	0.24	100%	$1,720,924	$0.02
Sales	$75,000	182.6	2.61	50%	$9,245,869	$0.13
Marketing	$75,000	27.7	0.40	100%	$2,808,872	$0.04
EPC sales management	$75,000	43.9	0.63	100%	$4,447,380	$0.06
Subtotal: employees		538.0	7.69		$43,535,891	$0.62
Benefits, FICA, bonus (added to base salary)	35%					
Total indirect corporate costs (staff + business expenses)					**$53,181,843**	**$0.76**
Direct Corporate Overhead						
Staff Expenses						
	Base Salary (unburdened) / person	# of employees	Employees per MW installed	Time assoc. w/direct proj. cost	(Base Salary + Benefits) × % of time	
Design and engineering	$75,000	66.4		50%	$3,359,415	$0.05
Project management	$75,000	42.5		90%	$3,872,078	$0.06
Sales	$75,000	182.6		50%	$9,245,869	$0.13

Total direct corporate staff costs	**$16,477,362**	**$0.24**
MW installed by developer per year	70	

Appendix C. Breakdown of Direct Costs and Margins

Table C-1. Breakdown of Direct Costs and Margins in 2012[23]

				Residential ($/W$_{DC}$)	Commercial ($/W$_{DC}$)
	Average system size (kW)[24]			5.1	221
Hardware, Construction Labor, Insurance, Permitting & Interconnection fees	Module	NREL Benchmarks		$ 1.03	$ 1.03
	Inverter			$ 0.43	$ 0.29
	Installation materials			$ 0.44	$ 0.63
	Installation labor			$ 0.55	$ 0.28
	Labor Benefits, FICA, bonus	35% of labor costs		$ 0.19	$ 0.10
	EPC direct staff costs	From *Table A-1* and *Table A-2*		$ 0.19	$ 0.15
	Permitting & interconnection fees	$430 Res., $5,000 Com.		$ 0.08	$ 0.02
	Construction insurance	0.3% fee on system price to integrator		$ 0.01	$ 0.01
	Subtotal: EPC Cost			**$ 2.92**	**$ 2.50**
	EPC margin	20% of cost res. 10% of cost com.		$ 0.58	$ 0.25
System Price to Developer				**$ 3.50**	**$ 2.76**
Direct Staff Costs by Developer		From *Table B-1*		**$ 0.24**	**$ 0.24**
	Average transaction size (MW In portfolio)			10	10
Transactional Costs	*Professional Services*	*$/Portfolio*			
	Developer legal fees	$	250,000	$ 0.03	$ 0.03
	Tax-equity legal fees	$	250,000	$ 0.03	$ 0.03
	Auditor (for residential only)	$	10,000	$ 0.00	N/A
	Accountants	$	25,000	$ 0.00	$ 0.00
	Independent engineering (for commercial only)	$	75,000	N/A	$ 0.01
	Subtotal: Professional Services			*$ 0.05*	*$ 0.06*
	Financier Expenses				
	Fees from term debt	2.5% fee on loan amount (40% of system price to developer)		$ 0.04	$ 0.02
	Fees from construction debt / revolving line of credit (for commercial only)	1% fee on loan amount (75% of system price to developer)		N/A	$ 0.02
	Interest on loan / line of credit (during construction, for commercial only)	5% interest rate on loan for 6 months		N/A	$ 0.04
	Subtotal: Financier Expenses			*$ 0.04*	*$ 0.08*
	Additional Costs				

---

[23] Columns may not add due to rounding.
[24] System sizes correspond with modeled hardware and labor costs

Inverter warranties (20 years)		$ 0.10		$ 0.09
System production guarantees		$ 0.02		$ 0.01
Subtotal: Additional Costs		*$ 0.12*		*$ 0.10*
Subtotal: Transactional Costs		**$ 0.21**		**$ 0.24**
Mark-up to tax equity in sale-leaseback structure	15% of all costs	**$ 0.57**		**$ 0.43**
Total System Price		**$ 4.52**		**$ 3.66**
Cash Reserves				
Debt service reserve	Reserve of 5% interest rate on term loan for 6 months (40% of total system price)	$ 0.04		$ 0.04
O&M reserve	6-month reserve of O&M costs ($23.5/kW, per year)	$ 0.01		$ 0.01
Total Cash Reserves		**$ 0.05**		**$ 0.05**
Total System Price Plus Cash Reserves		**$ 4.58**		**$ 3.71**

www.ingramcontent.com/pod-product-compliance
Lightning Source LLC
Chambersburg PA
CBHW081825170526
45167CB00008B/3545